At Least You Tried

Katy Byers

BookLeaf Publishing

India | USA | UK

Made with ❤ on the BookLeaf Publishing Platform
www.bookleafpub.in
www.bookleafpub.com

Dedication

For Sam, my biggest and sometimes only fan. Thank you for always making me want to be better, and being willing to grow with me on this adventure that is life. Let's keep feeling our feelings, even if it's not always easy.

Preface

"At least You Tried" is a collection of poems from the mind of a girl with little to lose and a lot of baggage. Exploring different emotions and experiences from working a job you hate to that regret of a love lost, "At least You Tried" has something for those of humanity that feel their feelings a little to hard sometimes. Never mind that I wasn't totally sure how to spell 'at least', you learn something new everyday. Sometimes you have to accept that you don't know anything. So let's get deep. Well, we'll at least try.

Acknowledgements

First, thank YOU. Thank you for picking up this book. The idea that my words are able to reach someone fills me with immense joy.

Forever grateful and forever thankful to the love of my life, Sam. Thank you for always supporting me even when I'm unable to support myself. Thank you for you patience, I know I'm not the easiest person to love. And thank you for loving me, your love has changed my life forever.

I wouldn't be who I am today without my parents. Dad, thank you for always wanting me to accomplish everything I wanted to. The discipline you tried to instill in me left great guilt, but there is nothing quite like guilt to make an anxious person get off their ass. Mom, thank you for always being a warm and loving person. You made me feel normal for the weird stuff I would get excited about and always entertained my silly desires. I am truly blessed to have parents like you.

To everyone else, you know who you are. Thank you for being my friend and thank you for dealing with the mess that is me. You keep me sane, happy, and feeling like I might actually have people I can talk to.

1. A Bother

Trying to get to the finish line
Trying to properly manage your time
Trying to keep the passion there
Trying to stay self-aware

Doing the work when it's no longer fun
Doing the crawl so later you run
Doing the things that you know you need to
Doing the things that they tell you to do

Having a breakdown, back the next day
Having desire to leave, only have enough energy to stay
Having to accept that the future is on you
Figuring out what you want to do.

2. Reckless Implusive

Having too many passions
Aways finding more
Wanting to be a master
Barely able to get off the floor

Learning a new skill
Giving up just as fast
Beating myself up for failing
Keep myself stuck in the past

Singing praises for others that try
but never any for myself.
Stuck between doing things for me
or just trying to accumulate wealth.

Maybe if I have more free time,
maybe if i had more friends,
maybe if i had more motivation
I'd finally reach the end.

3. Plenty of Fish

Fish come in a variety of shapes.
It's often easy to forget
that not every fish will be perfect for you,
some too big, too small for your net.

But all fish go through hardships,
they toss among the waves.
Losing patience or the ability to grant pardon
can be a grave mistake.

Just because you put a fish back,
that one was too red or too blue,
Looking at fish, it can be so easy to judge,
but don't forget that you're a fish too.

4. Stories to Tell

Tell me a story,
maybe one or two,
I wouldn't mind sharing some of mine with you.

Thank you for coming,
thanks for having me,
I'd spend time with you anytime baby.

I never want to leave
when you're so cuddly.
Next to you I can't sleep,
we stay up late so easily.

We kiss it's hard to breath,
how are you so pretty?
All the time, hard to believe
That you ended up liking me.

Let's karaoke,
let's stroll through the park,
I don't mind that it's almost getting dark.

Hold my hand lightly,
plant a kiss or three,

Sending shocks running through my whole body.

You act suspiciously
but that's ok with me.
Even as you torture me,
I'll thank you for it happily.

Each touch electricity.
If you know what you do to me.
Not just physically,
you're beautiful emotionally.

5. Our World is a Mess

You think you're funny?
You think you're smart?
You think you're deep
because you threw soup on art?

That guy's an entitled ass.
This guy pours oil on grass.
Enjoy the air while you can
before the atmosphere tanks from greenhouse gas.

The injustice hides
As consideration dies
while we pay for the next campaign
based on an agenda disguised with lies.

I'm not angry,
I've given up,
Why should I be the one to give a fuck?
Because someone has to.

6. Harry, Sally, Holt

Harry had to find a way
to figure out what he wanted to say
in a way that would not delay
the truth behind his feelings today

Sally didn't have trouble talking.
It came to her as natural as walking.
But that meant she was often interrupting
and to others that could be frustrating.

Holt didn't care much for others.
His inside circle included only his brother.
But he still made time for his mother
and he patiently searched for a lover.

Everyone has strengths and weaknesses.
Sometimes it takes time to find your uniqueness,
so go on, fight off the bleakness
and love yourself today.

7. Humans Want

People want to fly,
fly far far away
from their problems, from the drama
just to avoid their everyday.

The lives they live to pass the time
the jobs they keep to make ends meets
the friends that cause them trouble
the ones that call them weak.

Sadly humans don't have wings
or feathers to fly at all,
but close your eyes and count down from five
and maybe in your dreams you'll soar.

but why can't we live freely?
Why do we live to work?
To grind and spend our hours wisely,
on the back burner our dreams lurk.

But you can do it whenever,
you can choose to follow your dreams
then after living life for you for a while,
you can return them back to dreams.

Because the world is dumb like that
and we did it to ourselves.
We made the world what it is today
when we could be living for ourselves.

8. Run Jump Glide

Jumping high above the water where it's easier to
breathe,
but take a deep breath before plunging in the deep.

Gliding across ice is easier with skates,
but it's harder to pause, to put on the brakes.

Digging deep requires determination and grit,
but that doesn't guarantee you find any gifts.

Running faster means effort and effort takes time,
just getting to running meant crawling the line,

Living isn't easy but one thing is for sure
we can always find something worth fighting for.

Just look for it.

9. Birds Fly South

The birds fly south for the winter
to stay away from the cold.
To keep themselves safe from freezing,
to stay well fed and grow old.

Fish swim upstream to lay eggs
to continue their legacies.
Avoiding hazards as they can,
to make it to places that please.

Mammals do so much to survive
but still make time for fun.
Like rabbits playing chase all day,
leaping playfully in the sun.

All these creatures here on earth
and we have so many strides.
Through technology and medicine, AI and comms,
but really, we all need to ask why?

Why is there so much injustice?
Despite humans being so smart.
Why do we focus on silly unimportant things,
when humanity is losing it's heart?

Should we continue to allow greed to prevail?

Shall we keep trying to fight?

What would happen if we truly united?

What would happen in we erased our greedy plight?

10. Happiness is Fleeting

Happiness is fleeting,
don't forget to get your void filled.
Think that you found something
that convinces you that you're healed,

but in time
you'll find

everything is changing
nothing stays the way you want it,
Spend time growing and loving,
just to realize you've lost it,

That's how
you're found

Broken on the cold floor.
It's easy to ignore that every time
you close your eyes
you're losing more of the fight
that keeps you

alive.

11. Mirror Mirror

Mirror mirror on the wall,
why do you tease me so?

I want to see if I look nice,
but I know the answer is no.

So I leave without looking
and try to feel good despite

the lack of feeling confident,
of never feeling right.

I don't want to hate getting ready.
Shopping is no longer fun.

I hate everything that I put myself in.
Everyday I'm just ready to be done.

12. So Cold

How can you be so cold
when you just walked into the room?
Usually it takes time
for ice to build.

I don't want to be in a home that's not warm,
where I feel like I can't breathe.
It's not fair that you come at me with bad energy,
it's not fair the way you treat me.

I don't like it.
I don't want.
I don't think it's for me.

13. Hello?

Heaven calls to tell you that
you need to do better.
At this rate you're doomed to burn
down in hell forever.

Hell calls to let you know,
they don't want you either.
You're not badass enough to join,
so on this line you teeter.

Earth is calling, it sounds like hell,
it's easy to confuse the two.
Earth said that you're good right here,
don't leave yet, people still need you.

14. You Can Do It

Here I go, I can do it.
I tell myself that I can push through it.
But there's that voice in the back of my mind,
saying that I'll fail, you suck, maybe next time.

Failure isn't that scary.
I've failed in the past plenty.
What scares me most is the rejection,
those feelings hurt like an injection.

I used to think I was stronger,
tougher, wiser, a war mongerer.
But then my motivation left me
I wasn't Khan, I was Ghandi.

I'm starting to get it back now though,
after a long time of feeling low.
Sometimes it still gets me down,
but I always love to clown.

15. The Earth is Flat

The earth is now flat.
We are all connected.
Flat earthers were wrong,
my reach can go anywhere directed.

Friends across the globe.
Breaking news from France.
The north pole's melting even more
and rebels are taking a chance.

Its crazy how i can talk to you,
stream and game and chat,
and form these connections everywhere
at the drop of a hat.

Life would have been way harder
without access to the net.
How would nerds find each othcr?
How would we have met?

Oh well, lets not dwell on it.
Time keeps moving forward .
And with it technology, power,
and the tools to help you discover

You.

16. I Can Do It

As time rolls by and we get older,
nothing can change the fact that we're bolder.
We have more faith in ourselves
and we have more stories to tell.

Dance the night away to get to the next day.
Finding time to have fun, even if it requires pay.
Anything you can do, I'll try to be better.
Anything you can't do, I'll try that too.

17. Write Anyway

Didn't want to write today.
Didn't want to edit.
Didn't want to work the shift,
woke up and instantly dread it.

Had to force myself to eat today.
Had to fight to go to sleep.
Had lots of things I wanted to do,
but only managed a few things.

Decide to do somethings anyway,
even if they are small.
Each day, just choose to write anyway
despite hitting that mental wall.

18. Say Yes

Sometimes people struggle to find
a reason to go, to waste their time.
But each time you go, without fail,
you have no regrets, good times we nailed.

Everybody has to do things that are a bother.
Sometimes we have to say yes despite the falter.
But once you're done, you can sit back and relax.
Feels good to be productive, feels good to face the facts.

Say yes to that thing you're unsure of.
Say yes to what you say you love.
Say yes because maybe one day
saying yes will be easier to do then yesterday.

19. You're Human Too

People can be so hard on themselves,
but be the nicest person to literally anyone else.
Be forgiving, be sweet, be charming, a treat,
but can never say anything good about the person in the
mirror.

Think about who you used to be,
when you were young and still full of glee.
When you maybe weren't so hard on yourself,
when maybe you didn't always have to dwell.

Dwell on mistakes you made long ago.
Dwell on the things that make you cringe, make you cry,
say woah.
People make mistakes, it's only human,
so be a little nicer to that person you're bullying.

20. Distractions Everywhere

Pretty lights shining bright.
Televisions screens beckoning me.
Phone calls and text to make me forget
what the hell I was doing.

Dreams of fun days in the sun.
Wanting to get out, to leave the house.
Never wanting to wake up for a day of work stuff
but always having to do anyway.

Distractions from the things that bring us joy.
Needs that require your time and your fire.
So little left to take care of the rest
of the things you actually wanted to do.

21. The End

Before you know it, the time has passed.
Your art is complete, your checklist dashed.
You wonder why you struggled to make it through.
You wonder if maybe the problem was you.

Forget that thought, revel in the glory
Of being able to finally complete your story.
And when you're ready to show the world just what
you've been working on despite any brain hiccups.

Have pride in yourself and the things that you do.
Be as kind to yourself as you wish others were to.
When we stop holding ourselves back and just get it
done,
we can remember that we're human, all of us, everyone.

www.ingramcontent.com/pod-product-compliance
Lightning Source LLC
Chambersburg PA
CBHW071239140726
47996CB00007B/2673